THOMAS EDISON

Essential Lives

THOMAS

EDISON

BY CHARLES E. PEDERSON

Content Consultant
Louis Carlat, associate editor
Thomas A. Edison Papers, Rutgers University

ABDO
Publishing Company

JB
Edison ?

CREDITS

Published by ABDO Publishing Company, 8000 West 78th Street, Edina, Minnesota 55439. Copyright © 2008 by Abdo Consulting Group, Inc. International copyrights reserved in all countries. No part of this book may be reproduced in any form without written permission from the publisher. The Essential Library™ is a trademark and logo of ABDO Publishing Company.

Printed in the United States.

Editor: Jill Sherman
Cover Design: Becky Daum
Interior Design: Lindaanne Donohoe

Library of Congress Cataloging-in-Publication Data
Pederson, Charles E.
  Thomas Edison / Charles E. Pederson.
      p. cm.—(Essential lives)
  Includes bibliographical references and index.
  ISBN 978-1-59928-845-1
  1. Edison, Thomas A. (Thomas Alva), 1847-1931—Juvenile literature. 2. Inventors—United States—Biography—Juvenile literature. 3. Electric engineers—United States—Biography—Juvenile literature. I. Title.
  TK140.E3P44 2007
  621.3092—dc22
  [B]

                                                                2007012516

TABLE OF CONTENTS

Thomas Alva Edison

AN "ENLIGHTENED" INVENTOR

*I*t was a winter evening in late December 1879. As the steam engine pulled into the sleepy train station, the brakeman leaped along the train from car to car, twisting the brakes of each one. Each train car had a brake wheel on its roof that needed to be turned by hand to set the brakes. The steam whistle shrieked, announcing the arrival of another cargo of important businessmen, newspaper reporters, and members of the public.

The group was one of many who had traveled daily to visit the workshop of America's greatest living inventor, Thomas Edison. He and his group of thinkers and tinkerers had been developing a product for a number of years. Edison believed it would become an important part of everyday life in the United States and around the world. That invention was a practical electric light bulb. Edison did not invent the first light bulb or even the first electric light. He had aimed, however, to perfect the electric light and had worked for several years to that end. Today, he would show the results of that labor.

Night was falling, and the group wanted to reach Edison's home and laboratory before it became too dark. They were talking excitedly, wondering what they would see. What would a light bulb be like? How bright could one light bulb be?

"Practical men, with experience, and what I call 'horse sense' … are the men whom I like to welcome to my laboratory."[1]

— *Thomas Edison*

INVENTION FACTORY

Everyone had heard of Edison's "invention factory," up the street

from his house at the corner
of Christie Street and
Thornall Avenue. He had set
up this research facility in the
New Jersey countryside
specifically to bring his many
ideas into existence. His
previous inventions had made
him as famous as a rock star
or sports hero is today.
Recently, Edison's team of
inventors had turned their
considerable talents toward
finding the solution to light
bulb problems, which
included making the bulb
burn longer. When people
learned he was developing a
practical electric light bulb,
many doubted it could
be done.

Inventors all over the world had long been trying
to create a practical electric light. Some of those
experiments had been more successful, some less so.
Some researchers had been at it for many years

Thomas Edison developed most of his inventions in his West Orange, New Jersey, laboratory.

before Edison. Problems plagued these lights. They were powered by batteries, but batteries supplied power only briefly. Many of these early lights were arc lights. These produce light by causing an arc, or sending a spark of electricity over a gap between two electric terminals. Arc lights produce extremely bright light, which would be hard, for example, to use for reading a book. Also, the carbon rods that created the gap for the arc burned out after a short period of time. In Edison's mind, too-bright light and short-lived power sources and components meant arc lights were impractical for widespread use inside homes.

The Light Bulb

The New York Times described Edison's bulb: "The lamp which Mr. Edison regards as a crowning triumph is a model of simplicity and economy."[2]

As was typical, his restless mind continued to search for a way to invent a practical light. Edison had helped design and create many inventions during his career, following one single rule about their development: they had to be practical, something people would want to buy. If Edison believed an invention would not sell, he would not pursue it. Long before, he had decided the electric light bulb would be practical, useful, and desired by the public.

In 1878, a year before the December train carried its visitors to Edison's town, Edison and several other visitors had paid a call on William Wallace. Wallace's workshop had produced arc lights that were not

Thomas Edison's incandescent bulb was the first practical light bulb.

powered by batteries. The lights were powered by a generator, or dynamo, he had created. The generator, using magnets and coiled wires, changed mechanical energy into electrical energy. Wallace's system powered eight electric lights. The problem with Wallace's system, though, was that if one light burned out, none of the remaining lights worked. Imagine a house with eight rooms, and each room had one of Wallace's lights. If the light went out in the bedroom, the lights in the kitchen, garage, basement, and other rooms would also go out, leaving their occupants in the dark. Still, Wallace's demonstration proved a power source other than batteries could be used. Edison liked the idea of using an electromagnetic dynamo.

Edison began to experiment with glowing filaments rather than arc lights. A filament is a threadlike material that spans the gap between the rods of an arc light. When the filament is heated, it should gently glow and give off a muted light, perfect for indoor lighting. Edison's factory tested thousands of different materials

Steam Trains

The history of steam trains, such as the one Edison's visitors rode to his invention factory in Menlo Park, is a long one. Railroads had existed in Europe since the 1500s to pull coal and iron ore from underground mines. These early "railroads" were pulled by horses along wooden tracks. Gradually, iron rails replaced the early wooden rails these mines used. Around 1800, Richard Trevithick invented the first successful steam engine. George Stephenson opened the first freight railroad in 1825 and the first passenger service in 1830. Both used steam engines.

Railroads began running in the United States shortly thereafter. The first full-sized railroad in North America began running in 1829. After that, railroad companies opened systems all over the eastern United States. By 1836, more than 1,000 miles (1,609 km) of track had been laid, mainly in the eastern United States.

In 1869, the first tracks had crossed the United States, connecting the East Coast with newly settled areas along the Pacific coastline.

As the years passed, improvements in technology allowed diesel engines to replace the old steam engines. Today, these huge monsters can pull as many as 200 cars in a long train.

to create the filament. Some of these did not glow at all. Some glowed but quickly burned out. Finally, Edison settled on carbonized, or burned, thread. He also worked on the problem of keeping the other lights lit on a circuit if one bulb burned out.

A Successful Demonstration

When the group of Christmas visitors from the train left the tiny station, they could see Edison's home and Christie Street, which led to his research laboratory. The group stopped in their tracks, staring with astonishment. Electric streetlights lined the road, lighting the visitors' way. It was like a scene under a candlelit Christmas tree. The people could not believe their eyes. All these lights! Nearing their destination, the visitors were even more astounded by Edison's lab. About 25 light bulbs glowed inside. It seemed almost as bright as day.

In the coming days, people in the streets excitedly greeted the announcement of this successful demonstration. Newspapers trumpeted Edison's achievement. Investors who had funded Edison's dream

"I think it is always beneficial to put a little sentiment in business."[3]

—*Thomas Edison*

breathed a sigh of relief. Perhaps it would be practical to create a whole new industry based on this pear-shaped lump of glass after all.

"You must know that it takes considerable thinking and brains to carry on all these machines at once."[4]

— *Thomas Edison*

The gas-lighting industry reacted differently. Gas manufactured from coal had been used to light homes for many years. In these lamps, coal gas was ignited into a small flame. It burned within a glass globe attached to a room's wall. When Edison announced he would use electricity to light the country, stock prices for gas companies dropped steeply. However, those prices later rose again when it became clear Edison would not be able to light the entire country at once. Gas lighting would not disappear overnight.

Over the next few years, Edison and his invention factory worked hard to create everything needed for an entire electrical delivery system. The efforts of Edison and his coworkers brought the world from the gas-lighted past into the electrical world of the future. This Christmas showing, however, was the first practical incandescent light bulb. The visitors sensed the significance of Edison's accomplishment, which was already changing the world.

Because of Edison's work, entire cities could run on electricity.

Thomas Edison grew up in this house in Milan, Ohio.

EARLY LIFE

homas Alva Edison was born in 1847. That was a little more than 60 years after the American Revolutionary War (1775–1783) and about 40 years after Lewis and Clark explored the vast Louisiana Purchase.

In 1847, the United States had a much slower pace than it does today. The Industrial Revolution still had not taken firm hold on the country. Instead of many large industries, most of the country still consisted of small family farms and small businesses. Travel was difficult because paved roads between towns were rare. People rose with the sun, worked in daylight, and went to bed when darkness came.

In 1847, only 29 states made up the United States. Iowa had been the most recent admission, one year before. The United States was in the middle of the Mexican War (1846–1848). After the war, the United States gained large chunks of territory from Mexico. This area became California, Nevada, Utah, most of New Mexico and Arizona, and parts of Colorado and Wyoming. The Mexican War was minor compared to the U.S. Civil War (1861–1865). With this war, industry in the United States came into its own. To produce enough arms, ammunition, and other war materials, Northern industries quickly grew. Factories sprang up. Railroads were extended into a complicated web, covering the eastern part of the North American continent. Both North and South

"Without machinery society would drift into the condition of master and slave."[1]

— *Thomas Edison*

used the latest technology to gain their ends. In the North, the goals were to save the Union and to end slavery. The South opposed the federal government's intrusion on states' rights to govern themselves. They aimed to protect their agricultural life, including the use of slaves.

EDISON FAMILY HISTORY

The Edison family lived through these times. Thomas Edison's great-grandfather, John Edeson (pronounced AY-duh-suhn), was a Dutch farmer in New Jersey. During the American Revolution, he was a Tory. Tories were American colonists who opposed separating the colonies from Great Britain. Edeson continued to support the king of England, George III. At the war's end, many Tories did not stay in the United States. Many moved to Britain. Others, such as Edeson, were resettled by the British government in Canada. Not long after moving to Canada, the family changed the spelling of its name to Edison. The Edisons settled in Nova Scotia, on the east coast of Canada. Edison's grandfather, Samuel Edison, fought for the British during the War of 1812 (1812–1814). Edison's father, Samuel Jr., was born in Nova

Nancy Edison and her husband, Samuel, moved to Milan, Ohio,
to raise their family.

Scotia. He was mostly uneducated, moving from job to
job to earn money.

In 1828, Samuel Jr. met Nancy Elliot in Ontario,
Canada. They had little in common. She was the
daughter of a hero of the American Revolutionary
War, and her family was well respected in the United

States. She was as well educated and self-assured as any woman of the time and was not afraid to say what she thought. Samuel, on the other hand, had little education. His family had been on the losing side of the last two wars between Great Britain and the United States. Samuel and Nancy married in September 1828. For Samuel, it must have seemed like a step up in life.

Samuel and Nancy left Canada at the end of 1837. He had been a member of the "Mackenzie Rebellion" in Canada. In 1837, a group of men who called themselves Mackenzies attempted to overthrow the Canadian government. The group followed the American Revolution's protest against "taxation without representation." Unlike the American Revolution, the Mackenzies were unsuccessful in breaking away from Britain. Because Canada was part of the British Empire, the British government in Canada moved to crush the rebellion. The Mackenzie group members were forced to flee or risk being put in prison. Samuel and Nancy fled and eventually ended up in Milan, Ohio.

Milan, Ohio

Samuel was a hard worker, always looking to better his economic fortunes. Samuel's work life set an example that his son Thomas followed his entire life. On July 4,

1836, a canal opened in Milan, Ohio. Canals had been dug throughout the East to create better ways to get products from farms and factories to markets. The Erie Canal was the longest and most famous, completed in 1825. The Milan Canal ran from Milan to Lake Erie, one of the Great Lakes. From there, a ship could sail the lake's length to the Hudson River and the Erie Canal, eventually reaching the East Coast and markets much larger than those available in Milan. The canal transformed Milan into an inland seaport. In 1847, Milan was the world's second-busiest wheat-shipping port. Farmers from all over the area sold their wheat to be shipped east. Shipbuilding became a major industry in Milan.

Milan, Ohio

A writer described Milan, Ohio:

"It is an altogether pleasant and unpretentious town, which cherishes with no small amount of pride its association with the name of Thomas Alva Edison."[2]

Eagerly, Samuel entered these booming areas. He built a mill and a feed-grain store about 100 yards (91 m) from the canal. At the head of the mill, Samuel also built a sturdy home for his family. The house still stands today.

Samuel and Nancy began a large family. They had seven children, three of whom died in childhood. The youngest child was Thomas Alva Edison, born February 11, 1847. His life spanned the change from rural to urban, and from agricultural to industrial. He himself became a symbol of American hard work, "pulling himself up by his bootstraps" and becoming a self-made man.

CHILDHOOD

Edison's middle name came from a family friend, Alva Bradley. As a child, Edison was called Alva, or Al for short. He was seven years old when his family moved to Port Huron, Michigan, in 1854. There, he started school. After three months of school, the teacher punished Edison for not paying

The Erie Canal

Canals are waterways dug across dry land. They connect rivers and other bodies of water to each other. Canal boats, called barges, can carry much heavier freight than a wagon. Because canals are often straight, they can shorten a trip from place to place.

Among U.S. canals, the most famous was the Erie Canal. It crossed New York state from Buffalo, on Lake Erie, to Troy and Albany, on the Hudson River. From there, ships could reach New York City. The Erie Canal provided a way for goods and passengers from Buffalo to reach New York City without going through Canada.

Canal construction began in 1817 and was completed eight years later, in 1825. The canal was 363 miles (564 km) long. From Lake Erie to the Hudson River, the canal rose in steps about 560 feet (171 m)—approximately the height of a 60-story building! A series of locks created the steps. Locks were like big bathtubs with gates at both ends. A barge traveling upstream entered a lock, and the gates were closed. Water filled the lock, lifting the barge. When the water level in the lock matched the next one, the opposite gate opened.

attention. The teacher said Al was addled, or stupid. Based on his later life, Edison clearly was not stupid. However, little Al may have had trouble reading or the beginnings of hearing loss that came later in life. Nancy took Al out of the school and taught him at home. She encouraged him to read. Al read all kinds of books, from science texts to novels, and he kept the habit throughout his life.

> "My mother was the making of me. She was so true, so sure of me; and I felt I had someone to live for, someone I must not disappoint." [3]
>
> *— Thomas Edison*

By age nine, Al had read Richard G. Parker's *A School Compendium of Natural and Experimental Philosophy*. Parker was a famous teacher of the mid-1800s. The book had science experiments for beginners. Al found the experiments exciting and challenging. He performed all the experiments he could, and spent nearly all his allowance buying chemicals and supplies to perform them. He set up equipment in the corner of his home's basement to use as a lab. In 1976, excavations of the Edison home discovered "a large distribution of bottle glass and ceramic fragments in this heavily used vicinity."[4]

At age 20, Edison became particularly interested in the life and work of inventor Michael Faraday

(1791–1867). Faraday was involved in many experiments, particularly electrical experiments. His work inspired Edison, who performed the experiments he read about in Faraday's and others' books.

Edison was completely absorbed by these science books. He often blocked out all outside influences in order to focus on the task at hand. Edison's choice in life was to focus on his work rather than on a busy social life.

Edison enjoyed chemistry.

Thomas Edison, age 14

TEENAGE TELEGRAPHER

By the 1850s, the United States was energetic, ambitious, and ready to stand on its own. In many ways, Al shared that attitude. He, too, was eager to get out on his own and be independent. During Al's adult life, there was a popular U.S. author named Horatio Alger. He wrote stories about young boys who, through luck, optimism, and hard work, became rich and famous. As an adult, Edison also was able to overcome a lack of formal education to become one of the best-known Americans of all time.

Even as a youngster, Al showed the drive that would help him produce thousands of products during his life. By age nine, Al was growing vegetables on his father's farm. People living in Port Huron and riding the train were eager for fresh vegetables but did not have time to grow the food themselves. Al was so good at selling the food that he was able to hire two boys to assist with the business.

Always Thinking

Edison's mind was always dreaming up new ideas. His notebooks were filled with untested ideas. In one, he recommended applying nutrients to the skin after every washing to fight skin diseases.

When Al was a young boy, the U.S. rail system was just beginning. It had started mainly in the eastern United States and gradually extended west. By the 1850s, the railroad had reached Port Huron. Al was very excited by these "iron horses," as they sometimes were known.

GRAND TRUNK RAILROAD

At age 12, Al began to see the railroad industry close up. He got a job as a "news butch," selling newspapers on the Grand Trunk Railroad. This important rail line ran from Port Huron to Detroit, Michigan, stopping at towns along the way. It carried people who lived outside Detroit into the city, where they had jobs. In the evening, these workers traveled home along the Grand Trunk.

Along with newspapers, Al sold candy, apples, tobacco, and sandwiches. His job ran from 6:00 a.m. to 11:00 p.m. However, he was not on the train that whole time. He had long idle stretches. Whenever he could, Al spent hours reading at the Detroit library, and he read widely. Al read history, political philosophy, and fiction. Not surprisingly, he frequently read about physics and experimenting. He became an expert in mechanics and chemistry. It was during this time when Edison began to read about telegraphs and how they worked. Given his work schedule, he also became an expert at taking naps anywhere and at any time.

In 1862, at age 15, Al bought a used printing press and some used type. He began to publish the *Weekly Herald*. He created and printed this newspaper in an empty baggage car on the Grand Trunk. It was the first newspaper to be printed on a moving train. Al charged subscribers 8¢ a month. He printed train schedules and local news about towns along the line not otherwise covered in newspapers. He printed local gossip, birth announcements, and even jokes. One such joke went: "Let me collect myself, as the man said when he was blown up by a powder mill."[1] After only a few issues, Al lost interest in the newspaper and stopped publishing it. By age 15, he also decided he would rather be called Tom than Al.

Edison continued to sell the *Detroit Free Press* newspaper. Usually, he had 100 copies of the newspaper to sell to travelers. During the Civil War, he realized readers were more interested in the news than usual. During the Battle of Shiloh in 1862, for example, Edison bought 1,000 copies of the newspaper. Because so many people wanted a copy, he was able to raise the price of papers at each train stop. Normally costing 5¢, by the last stop, each copy was selling for 35¢.

About this time, Edison's hearing became much worse. As an adult, Edison told the story that he lost his hearing when a train conductor lifted him by his ears onto a train. Edison said he heard something snap. A more likely explanation is that Edison had scarlet

Edison on Music

Despite being hard of hearing, Edison enjoyed music:

"I seem to be gifted with a kind of inner hearing which enables me to detect sounds and noises which the ordinary listener does not hear."[2]

fever as a child. This disease mainly affects children, though not as seriously today as in Edison's time. Scarlet fever sometimes results in hearing loss. As an adult, Edison could hear only when people shouted at him. In fact, Edison claimed that the lack of hearing actually helped him concentrate while inventing. He had fewer distractions and could completely focus on one thing at a time.

The Telegraph

Edison continued to be fascinated by telegraphy, which provided a means for people to communicate over long distances. Telegraph operators,

---

The Telegraph

Samuel F. B. Morse made the first practical telegraph in 1837, only ten years before Edison was born. As with Edison and the light bulb, Morse did not invent the telegraph from scratch. He built on the work of earlier inventors.

Morse developed a code of dots and dashes. The dots were shorter electrical bursts. Dashes were longer. Originally, Morse wanted the combinations of dots and dashes to stand for numbers. Then the numbers would stand for words. A machinist named Alfred Vail began to work with Morse about 1837. Vail suggested that combinations of dots and dashes represent letters, not numbers. Together, Morse and Vail developed Morse code. For the most-often used letters, they used the simplest code. Rarely used letters have a more complicated combination of dots and dashes.

Shortly after its introduction, the telegraph became widely accepted. The first telegraph line ran from Baltimore, Maryland, to Washington, D.C. Less than 15 years after it was first introduced, more than 50 U.S. telegraph companies existed. News was sent over the wire, as well as military information during the Civil War and stock information after it.

or telegraphers, used Morse code. Using this series of long and short taps, telegraphers sent and received information along a wire stretched between telegraph stations. Edison hoped to become a telegrapher and taught himself Morse code.

Later, a telegrapher on the Grand Trunk, James MacKenzie, taught Edison telegraphy. One story says MacKenzie's son was playing on the rails and did not see a train coming toward him. Edison, however, did see the train. So did the train's brakeman, who quickly twisted the brake wheel. The train slowed enough to allow Edison to grab the child and save his life. As thanks, MacKenzie taught Edison telegraphy.

In the spring of 1863, Edison began work as a freelance telegrapher in Stratford Junction, Ontario, in Canada. This meant Edison was not a regular employee. His jobs usually lasted only a short time, and he moved from job to job for several years. Because he could only poorly hear the dots and dashes of Morse code, he had to "fill in the gaps." This meant guessing what messages were about if he missed parts of them. Luckily, Edison intently read newspapers and had a

Eating Habits

Edison had some odd eating habits: "I boil [all my food] except the water; no lettuce, celery or other raw things. The purpose of that is to guard me against bacterial invasion."[3]

good sense of politics and business. Filling in the gaps usually worked for him. Edison also created an automatic timed relay. Normally, a train worker sent regular messages to telegraphers to be sure they were paying attention. The telegraphers were supposed to reply. Edison's relay automatically replied to this message. Edison could then work on his own projects without interruption.

In addition to his poor hearing, Edison was also not the quickest telegrapher. A telegrapher usually wrote down messages immediately as they came in. If a message came in faster than the telegrapher could write, the telegrapher had to fill in the gaps. Edison got an idea for punching the message's dots and dashes onto paper tape. This let him copy the messages accurately, and at his own speed.

After a brief return to Port Huron, Edison became a telegrapher for the Western Union Telegraph Company. After briefly holding jobs here and there, he accepted a Western Union job in Boston, Massachusetts. Edison was excited about moving. At that time, Boston was the center of the invention world. Edison would begin his long and profitable career as an inventor there.

Thomas Edison at the telegraph

In Boston, Thomas Edison began to focus more on inventing.

Becoming a Full-time Inventor

Edison moved to Boston to work for Western Union in 1868. He hoped to learn more about and get into the telegraph industry. While in Boston, Edison continued to study and invent. He also continued his reading in the sciences.

One book he read was by Sir Isaac Newton, the famous English scientist and mathematician. The book's Latin title was *Philosophiae Naturalis Principia Mathematica* (*Mathematical Principles of Natural Philosophy*). This large volume was full of difficult mathematics. After reading the book, Edison decided he wanted nothing more to do with math. Faraday's work continued to influence Edison. Faraday's book *Experimental Researches in Electricity* described electrical experiments that fascinated Edison. Faraday's research methods and facilities also interested Edison. Perhaps most important, Faraday used no mathematics. Faraday was Edison's model for conducting experiments.

Edison continued to read about telegraphy. He had read books titled *Electrical Telegraph*, *Handbook of Practical Telegraphy*, and *History and Practice of the Electric Telegraph* while in Cincinnati, and he remained interested in the topic. He recognized that this fast means of communication was important, writing,

> "I have innumerable machines in my Mind now which I shall continue to illustrate & describe day by day when I have the spare time."[2]
>
> — *Thomas Edison*

The telegraph as a pivot-point marked the beginning of the end of nineteenth-century small worlds.[1]

First Patent

In Boston, Edison created his first patented invention. A patent is a document issued by the government that gives an inventor the rights to make and use an invention for a certain period of time. Patents protect inventors from having their inventions copied. Patents were always important to Edison. He often went to court to protect them.

Edison's invention was a vote counter for legislative offices. The vote counter would allow lawmakers to vote electrically, and record each vote on a chemically treated paper tape.

When Edison demonstrated the vote counter to congressmen in Washington, D.C., it worked perfectly. However, lawmakers did not like the vote counter. It sped up the voting process and reduced the amount of time they had to make deals or change their minds. Congress rejected the counter, and Edison could not sell it elsewhere. Edison learned never to create something unless people were willing to buy it.

Late Payments

Edison was not always prompt in paying his bills. A friend wrote, "On receipt of this you will immediately send the funds or write and give me some explanation of the matter. I am tired of writing about it and, if you can not attend to it, I propose to see if it can be collected."[3]

Afterward, in 1869, Edison left his job with Western Union and moved to New York City. He wanted to try inventing as a full-time job. However, he was not able to earn a living at first. He needed a job to support himself until he could open his own inventing firm.

POPE, EDISON, AND COMPANY

One day, Edison was waiting for a job interview at a company called Laws Gold Indicator Company. Laws used telegraphs to send information about the price of gold. The information left Laws' transmitter and went to bankers and stockbrokers around New York City. As Edison sat waiting, the office's central transmitting telegraph broke down. Edison learned of the broken transmitter and said he could fix it. He found the problem and corrected it. Laws' managers were so impressed at Edison's ability that they hired him. Eventually, he became the company's chief electrical engineer for $300 per month. This job gave Edison enough money to get settled in New York City.

In time, Edison formed his own company of electrical engineers: Pope, Edison, and Company. As with many of Edison's efforts, this was possibly a first—the first such firm of engineers. Their work was to:

... maintain and repair existing lines provided by other shops, install burglar and fire alarms, help draft patent applications for other entrepreneurs, and subcontract the expertise of [the owners] to purchase all manner of telegraphic supplies—cables, wire, insulators, as well as books.[4]

In late 1870, the Gold and Stock Telegraph Company paid Edison to create an improved stock ticker. Stock tickers used telegraph lines to send current stock prices to investors and stock sellers. Edison's financial backers expected quick results, but progress was slow. Edison reminded those investors that "no experiments are useless."[5] Edison believed every failure meant that the solution to a problem was that much closer. A collaborator of Edison's later wrote, "Edison is an indefatigable worker and there is no kind of failure however disastrous [that] affects him."[6] Eventually, Edison produced an improved stock ticker. He called it the Edison Universal Stock Printer. He sold the patents to Gold and Stock. He had hoped to earn $5,000 but was ready to accept as little as $3,000. Contrary to Edison's expectations, the owner of Gold and Stock offered him not $3,000 or even $5,000— but $40,000. Edison tried to act unsurprised as he accepted the offer.

The Universal Stock Printer was one of Edison's first successful inventions.

The money from Gold and Stock allowed Edison to quit his position with Pope, Edison, and Company and begin experimenting seriously. He leased laboratory space and began hiring collaborators. He became very successful and received about 200 patents over the next six years. Most of Edison's patents during this time were for improvements on existing telegraph equipment.

THE NEWARK FACTORY

In 1870, Edison left New York City and moved to Newark, New Jersey. Working in Newark, Edison became a full-time inventor. He set up a facility and began to collaborate with scientists and engineers. Edison taught himself the methods and operations of the industry that would make him a success. Edison's Newark factory helped make the city a center of invention. Edison called his building and operation an "invention factory." The Newark factory was Edison's first invention factory.

The pressure from financial backers to quickly

Robber Barons

The term "robber barons" refers to a group of wealthy financial leaders in the late 1800s and early 1900s. The robber barons were leaders in the industries where they made their money, often without seeming to care about their workers.

Robber barons included famous men such as John D. Rockefeller, Andrew Carnegie, and James J. Hill. Rockefeller's kingdom was the oil industry. Carnegie controlled the steel industry. Hill made a fortune in railroads. Each wanted to use the most efficient and modern technology, and each controlled a huge organization.

One of the most important robber barons was Jay Gould. Gould joined the board of directors of a railroad. He gained control of thousands of miles of rail lines. Gould sometimes used illegal means to become rich, both in railroads and in the stock market.

Gould wanted to control Western Union and did his best to stop competitors from besting him. Although not personally interested in Edison, Gould did use Edison's inventions as weapons in the fight for control of the telegraphs. Gould died of a lung disease in 1892, leaving his children a $77 million fortune (nearly $2 billion in today's worth).

finish products was heavy, and
Edison began to feel it, even as a
young man. By age 23, he claimed
that the stress of high-pressure
deadlines and meddling by his
financial investors had caused his
hair to turn white. He was most likely
exaggerating.

The Newark Laboratory

Edison bragged that his
Newark laboratory had
"every conceivable variety
of Electric Apparatus, and
any quantity of Chemicals
for experimentation."[7]

Charles Batchelor, among other
engineers and "mechanically talented
associates," joined Edison. Batchelor
remained one of Edison's longest-
lasting collaborators, working with
him for 25 years. He was an ideal worker for Edison,
preferring to remain in the shadows while Edison took
credit for his own and others' creations.

By 1874, Jay Gould, the railroad "robber baron,"
wanted to gain control of the telegraph industry. He
created a company to compete with Western Union.
Gould owned thousands of miles of railroads and the
surrounding property all over the United States. He
wanted to string wires along his tracks.

Gould's company bought smaller telegraph
companies and their patents and equipment. At the
time, Edison was working on a quadruplex telegraph

for Western Union. The quadruplex could send four messages at a time on one wire, instead of just one or two messages. This would save telegraph businesses money by increasing the number of messages that could be sent without requiring additional wires. According to one writer, the quadruplex "would bring dominance of the great industry to whoever owned it."[8] Gould wanted that dominance. Western Union had not paid Edison for his work, so Gould proposed to buy the quadruplex from Edison. However, once Gould gained control of Western Union, he did not need Edison's patents anymore. He could use any of the work Edison had done for Western Union. But Edison had still not been paid by Gould or Western Union. He sued both Gould and Western Union for payment. The lawsuit lasted for years before Edison was awarded payment.

Edison's Newark factory

Menlo Park invention factory

THE INVENTION FACTORY
AT MENLO PARK

By 1871, Edison had met and married his first wife, Mary Stilwell, and began to look for a larger home. In December 1875, he found one in the village of Menlo Park, New Jersey. In the late 1870s, Menlo Park was in the country. Edison biographer Neil Baldwin described the area:

> *On the height of the bluff [overlooking the Rahway River],*
> *in the country peace, crickets and tree-toads chirped, bees*
> *hummed, breezes blew, buttercups waved.*[1]

Edison wanted to continue to oversee his business affairs from there. The house was across the street from the railroad, making transportation to Newark and New York City easy. There was also land to construct a new laboratory.

MENLO PARK LABORATORY

Edison's research and inventions had begun to outgrow the Newark lab. He decided to build a new research facility. The property where he built the Menlo Park lab was perfect. It was about 12 miles (19 km) south of Newark and large enough that he could experiment all he wanted without disturbing his neighbors. In the spring of 1876, Edison moved the contents of the Newark factory into the factory he had built in Menlo Park. His house was about two blocks from the new factory, and the two buildings were linked by a telephone system.

Testing

Before hiring someone, Edison tested his knowledge. These tests were very difficult. Only 6 percent of the men who took the test scored a "Class A." Many failed the test entirely.

Located in New Jersey, Menlo Park was close enough to New York that Edison could keep in close contact with what was going on there, particularly regarding telegraphy. Western Union provided Edison with a connection to its main East Coast line, connecting him with Philadelphia and Washington, D.C. Menlo Park being on the rail line also made it easier for Edison to receive shipments and visitors and to travel to New York.

Honorary Degree

Edison received many honorary degrees. His first was awarded by Union College, Schenectady, New York.

To the visitors who approached Edison's home and laboratory, the rural setting must have seemed like a dream. Arriving through fields and villages, the visitors found a modern semi-industrial worksite. Neil Baldwin described the lab as being hung all over "with telegraph wires and lightning rods, with two brick chimneys rising from one side."[2] Edison's father had helped with the design and construction of the new buildings.

Edison wanted the labs at Menlo Park to be completely devoted to applying science and technology to solving problems of everyday life. He wanted practical products that would help people and earn him money. The many creations that came from Menlo

Park affected all areas of society and changed life worldwide. As the labs were built, Edison supervised every aspect of their design and construction.

NEW DEVELOPMENTS

In 1876, Edison had several important developments at Menlo Park. Western Union wanted Edison to develop a telephone to compete against Alexander Graham Bell's machine. Bell's telephone had poor sound quality, working only if the callers shouted. Edison decided to improve the sound quality by using a button made of carbon inside the machine as part of the transmitter. The carbon–button transmitter was immediately accepted. Edison's carbon button was used in all of Bell's telephones. This arrangement with Western Union and Bell confused the issue of who should receive money from the patent. Edison had created many inventions and sold the patents to Western Union. Because the company owned the rights to these patents, it decided to sell them to the Bell Telephone Company. In return, Edison received stock in Bell's company and a yearly amount of

"I am long on ideas, but short on time. I expect to live to be only about a hundred."[3]

— *Thomas Edison*

money. Edison was annoyed but could do nothing about the situation.

During this period, Edison produced his most popular invention, the phonograph. Edison got the idea for the phonograph while he was studying a telephone receiver. He saw that he could record sounds to be played later using some of the devices in a telephone. Edison made a sketch of how he envisioned the machine. He gave it to Charles Batchelor and John Kruesi, who worked in the invention factory, and told them to make it work. The two men translated Edison's idea into a working machine.

At the machine's first test, Edison recited the poem "Mary Had a Little Lamb." To the delight of the group

The Tasimeter

The tasimeter was a handheld instrument made of brass. It had a carbon button similar to the one Edison used in telephones. When heat was focused onto the button, it expanded and registered the heat change on a tiny screw. The screw was connected to a meter that showed the heat differences. The tasimeter was similar to a thermometer but much more sensitive. Later experiments confirmed that the tasimeter could measure temperature changes as small as one ten-thousandth of a degree Fahrenheit (–17.778° C).

Edison imagined many practical applications for the tasimeter. He imagined it could be used to take body temperatures, measure wind velocity, and detect smells, among other uses. Unfortunately, the "machine was too fickle, delicate, and overly sensitive to touch and vibration to serve any broader utilitarian purpose," he wrote.[4]

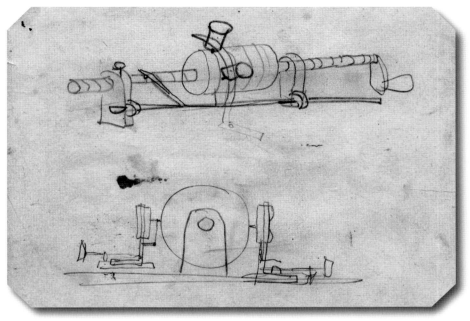

These sketches show Edison's plans for the phonograph.

watching—including Edison—they heard Edison's voice recreated exactly as he had just said it. With the announcement of this invention, Edison became known as the "Wizard of Menlo Park." He became famous the world over. Newspapers could not get enough of Edison. Some of the names the newspapers dreamed up for Edison included "Professor" Edison, "the New Jersey Columbus," and "the Napoleon of Invention."

Edison first publicly demonstrated the phonograph in the offices of *Scientific American* magazine. The machine delivered a brief message asking about the health of the listeners. The people in the room could scarcely believe their ears as they clearly made out the message and recognized Edison's voice.

"My philosophy of life is work, bringing out the secrets of nature, and applying them for the happiness of man. I know of no better service to render during the short time we are in this world."[5]

— *Thomas Edison*

Edison filed a patent for the phonograph in 1877. For many years, the phonograph was Edison's favorite invention. He predicted many practical uses for it. However, Edison soon became preoccupied with another invention that demanded his full attention.

In the summer of 1878, Edison was invited to join a scientific trip to the Rocky Mountains to measure a solar eclipse. Edison was to test out one of his inventions, a device to measure heat changes, called a tasimeter. During the trip, Edison began to think about electrically lighting entire cities. He returned to Menlo Park determined to create his own electric light.

The phonograph was Edison's favorite invention for many years.

Chapter 6

Thanks to Edison's work, electricity would one day light cities.

A Light Turns On

dison stated that he wanted to invent something new every ten days. For many years, he actually outdid that goal, averaging one new invention every five days. From 1876 to 1884, Edison applied for more than 400 patents from Menlo Park. These were mostly for electricity-related gadgets.

THE FIRST ELECTRIC LIGHTS

Though Edison made many inventions and improvements, today he is best known for his development of the incandescent light bulb. An incandescent bulb creates light when a filament, or fine thread, of a material is heated until it glows. The filament is placed inside a glass globe from which all air has been removed. This keeps oxygen away from the filament, so it does not burn up. Being in this vacuum helps the filament glow longer before burning out.

Edison rarely "invented" anything from scratch. Usually, he improved others' inventions. The same is true of the light bulb. In fact, the search for an electric light had been going on in Europe and the United States for several decades. The first electric arc lights had been attempted as early as 1802, only 20 years after the United States won the Revolutionary War. The first attempts to create incandescent light inside glass bulbs had begun around the 1840s. Joseph Swan, an Englishman, had experimented with carbonized materials inside a glass globe. He had begun in earnest to seek a reliable light bulb a few years before Edison

"The electric light is going to be a great success. I have something entirely new."[1]

—*Thomas Edison*

began his experiments. Hiram Maxim had applied for U.S. patents on his own version of a light bulb in 1879.

The problem with all these early light bulbs was that, though successful, their creators thought about them only on a small scale—for a limited number of light bulbs. Edison distinguished his attempts by envisioning not only a safe, practical, reliable light bulb but also an entire system to create, measure, distribute, and sell the electricity to light it.

Arc lighting had already been used to illuminate lighthouses and public gathering spaces. Still, these systems were too large and

Joseph Swan

Joseph Swan was an English chemist and inventor. In the 1840s, Swan began to experiment with electric lights. Like Edison, he wanted to find a practical means of indoor lighting. He experimented with filaments for 20 years. He had two problems. First, filaments worked better in a vacuum, but a pump to remove all air did not exist. Second, the batteries that supplied electricity were unreliable for lighting.

In the late 1870s, more efficient vacuum pumps were invented. By then, dynamos provided a better supply of electricity than batteries. Swan resumed the search for electric "glow bulbs," as he called them. Soon, he could light his own home with his bulbs. The lights became popular and were used in several important buildings in London.

At the same time, Edison was working on his light bulb, which he had patented. Edison sued Swan, but the lawsuit did not stop him. In 1883, the two settled out of court. They merged their companies, creating the United Electric Light Company, known as "Ediswan." The men controlled the production of light bulbs in Great Britain.

impractical for widespread household use. In 1878, Edison announced he would create practical electric lighting. His announcement caused a severe drop in gas stock prices. Coal gas (gas given off when coal is burned) had been one of the main ways to light homes in the 1800s. However, the gas was messy, creating a black soot that settled everywhere in a home, including on clothes, furniture, and the globe that contained the gas burner. It also was dangerous, using up oxygen and polluting the air, and sometimes causing fires.

"I never did anything worth doing by accident … No, when I have fully decided that a result is worth getting, I go ahead on it and make trial after trial until it comes."[2]

— *Thomas Edison*

On November 15, 1878, the Edison Electric Light Company was founded. Edison began seriously trying to solve the puzzle of practical electric lighting.

CREATING AN INCANDESCENT BULB

Edison quickly realized that the main problem of electric light bulbs was creating a filament that would last. The most common filament in Edison's day was made of platinum. It glowed but used a lot of electricity. Edison wanted a filament with higher resistance so less electricity would be required to make it glow. He made longer and thinner filaments, which increased the resistance, but they still did not work well. He turned to carbonized materials, which his lab was already using in telephones, wires, and batteries.

Edison instructed his employees to begin testing all sorts of materials to determine their resistance and ability to withstand high temperatures. In 1878, Edison hired Francis Upton for his understanding of physics and mathematics. The two men tried everything they could think of, including plant fibers, cardboard, paper, and even fishing line. They eventually discovered that carbonized cotton thread could burn for several hours before burning out.

As Edison's employees searched for the proper filament, he turned his attention to creating an efficient vacuum pump. Creating a vacuum meant removing all the air molecules from inside the glass bulb. With no air, the filament could glow longer because there was no oxygen to feed the burning element. However, the vacuum pump Edison was already using could not remove all the air from the bulb. In the glassblowing center on the Menlo Park property, he had one of his glassmakers create a new, more efficient pump.

On October 21, 1879, Edison and some of his employees were set to give another light bulb a "life test." This would determine how long the filament would glow before burning out. None of the men had any expectations for success with this bulb. They had already performed hundreds of similar tests without finding a filament that was suitable for long-lasting incandescence.

Overnight, Edison and one of his employees kept watch on the bulb, while other workers went home. When they returned the next day, the other workers were surprised to find that the light bulb was still glowing brightly. Edison and his men felt that they were on the right track.

Edison felt certain he was near to making a perfect light bulb. He announced his success to the public, who reacted with great excitement. Newspapers wrote endless numbers of articles about the Wizard of Menlo Park. Hundreds of people traveled by train to the Menlo Park factory every day. They were anxious to see the lighting display Edison had set up on the streets of

Electricity Supply

Edison was most interested in creating a system to supply electricity to cities, saying, "My idea is to have central stations to cover, say a square of three or four blocks. The pipes containing the wires on a street … They will be laid under the flag-stones just at the edge of the side-walk, as gas-pipes are laid now."[3]

the town and on the grounds of his laboratory. So many people traveled to Menlo Park to see Edison that extra trains were scheduled to handle them all. By 1880, Edison's lab had created a bamboo filament that could glow for more than 1,000 hours before burning out.

Lighting a City

Edison also designed an entire electrical storage and delivery system. Parts of this system he created were sockets, switches, fuses, junction boxes, lamp fixtures, and better dynamos. A dynamo turns mechanical energy (such as a spinning turbine wheel) into electrical energy. Edison charged one of his men with creating a dynamo large enough to supply electricity to many light bulbs on a large system. The worker created "Jumbo," a huge dynamo that could supply the energy Edison required. It was so large that it shook the ground when it was running. This dynamo was able to turn nearly 90 percent of its mechanical energy into electrical energy, where most dynamos of the time were about 40 percent efficient. Eventually, six Jumbo dynamos were created and moved to New York City. There, Edison wanted to turn electrical power into an everyday commodity for sale to anyone who wanted it.

He also created electrical meters to measure an individual's electricity use and charge them for it. He wanted cheap electricity, but he did not want to give it away for free.

Edison began to work in New York City to light parts of Manhattan. In September 1882, Edison opened the Pearl Street electrical generating station. Edison helped dig trenches from the station to lay underground wires. Eventually, more than ten miles (16 km) were laid. In 1883, Macy's department store became the first U.S. business to use electric incandescent light bulbs. Edison Electric Light Company eventually combined with several other of Edison's electrical companies to become Edison General Electric Company. In 1892, the Edison name was dropped to become simply General Electric Company, a company that still exists today.

Edison's system worked on a direct current (DC). Nikola Tesla, a former employee of Edison, tried for years to convince Edison that an alternating current (AC) would be better. Its voltage could easily be raised to allow electricity to be delivered over miles of wire. It could then be put through transformers to lower the voltage, making it safe for household use. Edison's system could serve only a few city blocks using DC.

AC versus DC

Edison wanted to use only direct current (DC) for delivering electricity. He waged a long fight against George Westinghouse, a fellow inventor, who was in favor of alternating current (AC). To show how dangerous AC was, Edison used it to electrocute several animals.

Eventually, Tesla left Edison to work for competitors. Edison never forgave him for that and worked hard to convince the public that DC was better. Edison was convinced that maintaining a lower voltage current would be much safer for the public. In spite of Edison's opposition, Tesla's alternating current became the industry standard and is still used in the United States.

It took Edison four years and 20,000 experiments to perfect the light bulb. Creating the bulb demonstrated his patience and experimental abilities. Even more clearly on display was his ability to envision an entire system of producing, storing, and delivering electricity.

Thomas Edison's dynamo made commercially generated electricity possible.

Edison (right) poses with Madeleine, Mina, Theodore, and Charles.

FAMILY MAN

Edison was close to his parents. He may
have wanted a similarly close relationship
with his wife and children. However, his ambitions
and interest in research and experimentation
sometimes made him a less-than-ideal husband
and father.

Despite his family attachments, after Edison left home, he had little contact with his parents. This was due to poor transportation, not because of a bad relationship with them. Unlike today, there were no automobiles or airplanes that could carry passengers long distances in short periods of time. Most people still walked from place to place, or they drove a wagon or rode a horse if they were wealthy. Trains were more common for long distances, but even a trip by train could be very slow. Once a person left home, close family contact was sometimes difficult, if not impossible. Even letters could take weeks or months to move from one part of the growing United States to another.

"I chew [tobacco] all the time. ... I had no end of trouble with Mrs. Edison about it and was on the point of quitting when I found out that the Chief Justice of the United States used tobacco in that way. I told Mrs. Edison and that let me out."[2]

— *Thomas Edison*

In early 1871, when Edison was 24, his mother died. Although she had been ill for some time, it must have been difficult for him. Edison felt she had been the guiding light of his childhood. Edison's father would die 25 years later in 1896 at age 92, claiming,

I have smoked and drank whisky moderately when I needed, and have known when to let it alone.[1]

Mary Stilwell

Edison met Mary Stilwell while she was employed in one of his businesses. She was 16 years old, while Edison was 24. Edison asked Mary's parents, Nicholas and Margaret Stilwell, for permission to marry her. Her parents said the two must wait because of the difference in their ages. Edison agreed, but they married later that year on December 25, 1871.

Although they seemed a good match—both having come from working-class backgrounds—the two did not have a completely happy marriage. Though he married, Edison changed few of his bachelor ways. He worked up to 100 hours a week. He often lived more at his lab than at home. He seemed almost unsure of what to do with Mary. Edison even left Mary alone on their wedding day to return to some important work at his laboratory.

Edison seems to have been unaware of what he should expect from his new wife. In fact, he seemed genuinely surprised to learn that Mary would not be joining him in his work. In one of his notebooks, Edison complained, "My wife Dearly Beloved Cannot invent worth a Damn!"[3]

Mary seems to have been a shy woman, and it is unclear if she had many friends of her own. In addition, although Edison earned a considerable amount of money, he spent most of it on supplies and equipment for his work. He was a poor money manager, waiting until the last minute to pay his bills. This may have distressed Mary. Edison was so involved in his own interests that it is possible he did not notice that Mary was unhappy.

Although Edison did not seem to notice Mary's unhappiness, the two did start a family. Marion Estelle was born in 1873. Edison called her "Dot," for one of the sounds made in Morse code. Thomas Alva Jr. was born in 1876. Naturally, Edison called him "Dash," for the other Morse code sound. William Leslie, a second son, joined the family in 1878. Edison enjoyed spending time with his family and meant to spend Sundays with them. Despite his good intentions, though, those Sunday family times rarely occurred.

To help care for the children and to keep Mary company, Mary's sister, Alice, came to live with the Edisons. She stayed with the family for several years until she married one of Edison's employees, a glassblower named William Holzer.

Mary became sick with scarlet fever. Her health quickly deteriorated, and she died in 1884 at age 29.

MINA MILLER

In 1885, Edison met a young woman named Mina Miller. She was the daughter of an inventor of agricultural harvesting machines from Akron, Ohio. Although the age difference between 19-year-old Mina and 38-year-old Edison was even greater than it had been with Mary, Mina seems to have been a better match for Edison. She was well-educated and had grown up with money. She was used to entertaining guests and knew how to behave in society.

Edison taught Mina how to communicate in Morse code. They sometimes used this skill to communicate secretly when others were around. In fact, Edison claims he tapped the following question into her hand: "Will you marry me?" She signaled back into his hand, "Yes." Edison was elated.

After their honeymoon in Florida, Edison and Mina moved into the Glenmont Estate. Located in West Orange, New Jersey, Glenmont sat on 14 acres (5.6 ha) of land. It was large enough for Edison's new wife and his three children. With a new mother for his children, Edison

"Saw a lady who looked liked Mina—got thinking about Mina and came near being run over by a street car—If Mina interferes much more will have to take out an accident policy."[4]

— *Thomas Edison*

Mina Miller and Thomas Edison

turned over most of their upbringing to Mina. As she was less than ten years older than Marion, this was difficult for Mina. Later, Marion Edison wrote of her stepmother that she was "too young to be a mother but too old to be a chum."[5]

In time, Mina and Edison had three more children: Madeleine, born in 1888 (she had Edison's only grandchildren); Charles, born in 1890; and Theodore, born in 1898. Mina's life away from Edison was more active than Mary's had been. She led many social clubs and supervised the busy Edison household.

Edison even put Glenmont in her name so creditors could not seize it if Edison went bankrupt.

CHILDREN

All the older Edison children attended boarding school, perhaps because Mary had found it hard to raise them herself. On the other hand, perhaps Edison did not want to be bothered with them.

As an adult, Thomas Jr. tried to use his famous last name to sell dubious inventions. This so enraged Edison that he made his son change his name. Thomas Jr. used "Thomas Willard" from that point forward. Late in life, Thomas tried farming, but that proved unsuccessful as well.

Charles Edison

Charles had the most in common with his father. Both men enjoyed fishing and cars. Charles worked on Edison's electric cars and drove with his father into the countryside.

Charles's school grades ranged from average to terrible. Nonetheless, Charles entered the Massachusetts Institute of Technology (MIT), near Boston. His father wanted him to study science, expecting him to enter the family business, but Charles never graduated.

In the 1930s, Charles entered politics. He assisted his father on the Naval Consulting Board. Franklin D. Roosevelt appointed Charles assistant secretary of the Navy in 1937. In 1940, Charles was elected governor of New Jersey, serving for several years.

Charles became president of Thomas A. Edison, Inc. He died in 1969. He once said,

> I have ... been faithful to the family tradition: I don't go looking for battles, but I always seem to be in one.[6]

Little William was a wild sort of child, "suspiciously resembling a chip off the old block."[7] His behavior caused problems between him and his father. Will, too, tried agriculture. All three of Edison and Mary's children eventually married but later had marriage problems.

Edison's three children with Mina seem to have fared better. Madeleine was a bright child who might have gone into the family business. However, women were not welcomed in the business world at that time. She was independent, even running for Congress (though unsuccessfully). She left money in her will to fund the Edison's Birthplace Museum in Milan, Ohio.

> "This sense of urgency was always present with us, but subconsciously so that it was not until I married and came back for visits that I realized under what constant pressure we lived at home."[9]
>
> —*Madeleine Edison*

Charles had the most successful public life of the Edison children. He did enter the family business. In late 1913, "in accordance with a long-held family understanding, Charles joined the payroll of Thomas A. Edison, Inc."[8] Charles worked his way up to become president of the company. Remembering his days as a laborer, Charles raised wages and shortened work hours. Charles enjoyed the arts. He started a theater group and a literary magazine in New York City.

Charles Edison on His Father

Edison's son Charles wrote to his famous father, "We have had our battles & differences of opinion but when all is said & done, you will stand out for me as the 'World's Best Sport.'"[11]

Charles began "to cast a small shadow of [his] own,"[10] away from his father. He served in the cabinet of Franklin D. Roosevelt and was later elected governor of New Jersey.

Theodore also entered the family business. He earned a college degree from the Massachusetts Institute of Technology (MIT). He was the only one of Edison's children to earn a college degree. He later started his own engineering company and earned more than 80 patents of his own.

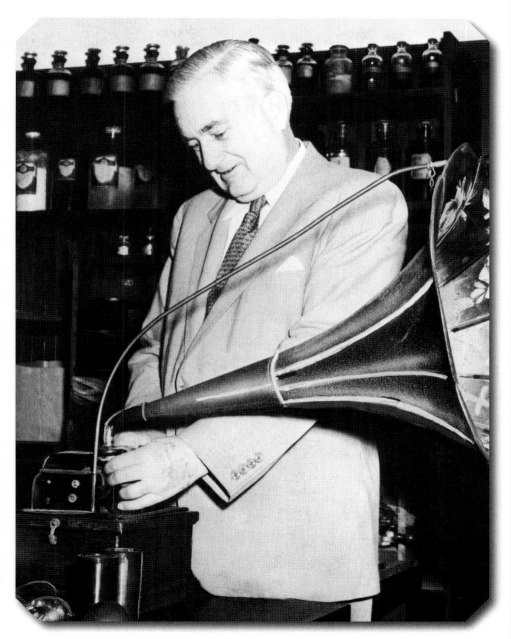

Charles Edison

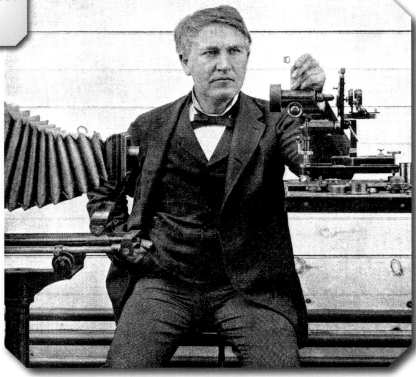

Thomas Edison poses with his kinetoscope.

THE WEST ORANGE YEARS

In only a few years, several hundred light bulbs had been installed at Menlo Park. After improving the light bulb, Edison and his group had to create from scratch the entire electrical generating, storage, and delivery system. For the next couple of years, Edison and his employees worked almost night and day to create these systems. As they did, Edison quickly incorporated the systems into Menlo Park.

Developing the light bulb and electrical systems meant increased work. Edison had to hire additional scientists and engineers to help develop his new ideas. After Edison and his research group had been in Menlo Park several years, the number of employees, equipment, and experiments had grown considerably. The Menlo Park laboratory no longer seemed large enough to hold everyone. Edison decided it was time for a larger research facility.

In the late 1880s, Edison began constructing yet another research facility in West Orange, New Jersey. This lab consisted of a main research building and several specialized research facilities. When completed, the Edison lab was the largest research facility in the world. Edison biographer Neil Baldwin noted that Edison kept all supplies on hand that he could think of for "anything and everything he needs or imagines he needs in practical or hypothetical situations."[2] These supplies included:

"My ambition is to build up a great Industrial works in the Orange Valley starting in a small way and gradually working up— The laboratory supplying the perfected inventions, models, patterns & fitting up necessary special machinery in the factory for each invention."[1]

— Thomas Edison

... skins of animals and feathers of birds, raw and tanned hides, minerals and precious stones, species of dried grasses and herbs, gums and spices in addition to the more conventional materials, chemicals, sheet metals, hardware of every shape and size, screws and bolts and angle-irons.[3]

Edison wanted to be prepared to act on any inspiration that might come his way.

According to some sources, the West Orange research laboratory was ten times as large as the Menlo Park lab. The facilities eventually spanned 21 acres (8.4 ha) and were frequently expanded to fit Edison's needs. Factories were built near Edison's laboratory to manufacture many of his inventions. At one point, about 10,000 people were employed there, and Edison himself practically lived there.

At West Orange, Edison began to rethink the phonograph. He had neglected it for many years, but competitors believed it could be improved and sold commercially. Most notably, Alexander Graham Bell created a version of the phonograph based on Edison's. This competition spurred Edison to return to the phonograph. His original broke down often and he believed he could improve the sound quality. He replaced the tinfoil-covered cylinder with a reusable wax cylinder that provided better sound quality. He also figured out a method to produce large numbers of the cylinders at a single pressing. A master metal plate held a negative of the original. This plate could be pressed into many new cylinders at the same time. To attract buyers, Edison had his phonographs hand-painted. Always good at sales, he had popular singers and musicians record music that people would want to buy.

"I have my own ideas, and I take my stand upon them, you know. A man who does that is always charged with eccentricity, inconsistency, and that kind of thing."[4]

— *Thomas Edison*

Edison dreamed up additional uses for phonographs. He believed their best use would be as dictation machines. He also thought about using them to record telephone conversations. He created a doll with an attached phonograph, so the toy could "talk." He considered the phonograph for:

> ... *letter writing and other forms of dictation; reading books for the blind; ... singing children to sleep; preserving "sayings, voices and last words of great men"; ... clocks that could tell you the hour of the day* ...[5]

Edison came to think so highly of his phonograph and its popularity that he called it "my baby." In fact, he nearly found it more important to him than his own real babies. When Mina and Edison had their first child, Madeleine, he left his work only briefly to see the infant. Although Edison adored Madeleine, he returned as soon as possible to what seemed the more pressing matter.

The phonograph was used for another purpose that created a separate industry of its own. Edison tried to synchronize, or match, the speech from a phonograph with moving pictures in a kinetoscope. This was a cabinet containing a roll of film with a series of photographs. A

Mesabi Iron Range

Part of northern Minnesota is known as "the Range." This name refers to the iron-mining region located there. The Mesabi Range is part of the region. The other parts are called the Vermilion and Cuyuna Ranges. The word *mesabe* comes from an Ojibway Indian word meaning "sleeping giant." Few white Americans cared about the area until iron ore was discovered there in the late 1800s. Unfortunately for Thomas Edison, the discovery came shortly before he began to process low-grade iron ore in the east.

The Mesabi Range holds iron ore, which is a rock containing iron. The technique used to mine the ore is called open-pit mining. The rock, dirt, and other materials covering the iron-bearing rock are stripped away. Then the ore is blasted into horizontal layers. These layers act like roads on which large trucks carry away the loosened ore. Then the ore is shipped for processing.

By 1900, more than 100 open-pit mines were operating on the Range. From 1900 to 1980, about 60 percent of U.S. iron ore came from the Range. Today, most of the Range's high-grade iron ore has been mined.

person looked through a hole at the running film, which gave the illusion of movement. The kinetoscope was the beginning of the movie industry. West Orange had a film studio called the Black Maria. It was covered outside with tar paper but had a movable roof to let in light. The studio rested on a circular track so it could be turned to follow the sun as needed for natural light.

Edison patented much of the equipment used in the early film industry. Imitators were quick to copy those inventions. Edison strongly defended his patents, and he was quick to bring people to court when they tried to steal them. Many of those he sued left for other areas of the country, including Hollywood. They did so to protect themselves from Edison's lawyers. These filmmakers found that Hollywood suited the industry perfectly. As Edison lost interest in making movies, the Hollywood producers took over, building the industry known today.

During the 1890s, the steel industry was one of the largest in the world, and the U.S. steel industry in

Kinetoscope

Not everyone appreciated the kinetoscope. A Texas law required all pictures be screened to be sure they were not "calculated to corrupt the morals of the youth, calculated to incite or provoke racial prejudices and create disorder, or so vulgar, obscene and indecent as to offend and demoralize public decency."[6]

particular was growing and powerful. Edison began to believe it would be profitable to figure out how to mine low-grade iron-containing rock, or iron ore, and process it cheaply into high-grade ore. He conducted experiments and set up a full-scale processing plant in northern New Jersey. He brought rocks from the mines to the plant. There, conveyor belts carried the rocks along the processing path. Giant crushers turned the iron-bearing rocks into dust. Then he used equally large electromagnets to pull the iron ore from the dust.

The technology worked well, but the business failed anyway. Unfortunately for Edison, large reserves of high-grade iron ore were discovered in northern Minnesota. The ore in the Mesabi Range was close to the earth's surface. It was easily mined and cheaper to process than the iron Edison took from the ground in the east. He lost all the money he had invested in the process. It was the largest commercial failure of his life.

Created with the kinetoscope, these images of a man sneezing
became one of Edison's first moving pictures.

Thomas Edison reads at his Glenmont Estate in West Orange, New Jersey.

LATER LIFE

After the failure of his mining company, Edison believed the next big thing would be producing Portland cement. This gray powder is mixed with gravel to make concrete. To produce cement, he used the technology developed for his mining ventures. Many building projects in

New York City and elsewhere used Edison's cement. These projects included large factories and even the original Yankee Stadium.

In the early 1900s, Edison began to broaden his horizons again by developing an electric car. He thought horse-drawn vehicles were on the way out. He believed "horseless carriages" would be the transportation of the future. His huge dynamos and electrical systems showed that electricity was reliable. The only thing needed to make electric cars a reality was a practical small battery that could store electricity and be recharged. Batteries that had been built up to that point, however, did not last long. They contained lead and acid, which leaked and became drained of power quickly.

"These batteries will run for 100 miles (160 km) or more without recharging. … I do not know how long it would take to wear out one of the batteries, for we have not yet been able to exhaust the possibilities of one of them."[1]

— *Thomas Edison*

Edison decided to develop a totally new type of battery using materials other than acid and lead. Having hired a large work force, he began to experiment. To Edison, working on the project was similar to his work at the Menlo Park factory. He stayed up until all hours of the night repeating hundreds of experiments. Edison said that when the number of experiments reached into the tens of thousands, "they turned the register back to zero and started over again."[2]

He then went on to build several early electric vehicles that he used at his Glenmont estate. Experimenting with different combinations of chemicals, he was eventually able to develop a practical battery for them to run off. However, gas-powered autos as built by Henry Ford eventually won out. Still, the battery Edison developed for cars had many other applications, such as use in train signals and safety lighting for mines. Eventually, the storage battery became his most profitable invention.

"The Government should maintain a great research laboratory. ... In this could be developed ... all the technique of military and naval progression without any vast expense."[3]

— *Thomas Edison*

During World War I (1914–1918), Edison led the Naval Consulting Board. His job was to examine inventions that were meant to help the military. Edison used the opportunity to earn as many as 40 patents. His patented inventions included equipment to help ships navigate, smoke screens to protect ships, underwater searchlights, and weapons-aiming systems. He also developed an electric lantern used in mining operations.

Edison rides in his first electric truck in 1923.

After the war ended, Edison wanted to return
to research and let someone else run his companies.
His son, Charles, had been involved in Edison's
company for some time and had worked his way up
in the company. Edison decided Charles was ready
to take over the day-to-day operations and so turned
that task over to him.

In the 1920s, Edison took several trips with his friend, Henry Ford, the famous auto manufacturer.

The Four Vagabonds

Beginning in 1916, Edison and three friends took a trip nearly every year. The friends were nearly as well-known as Edison. They included Henry Ford, who had once been an employee of Edison. Ford later became wealthy producing automobiles. Harvey Firestone was a rubber tycoon. He teamed up with Ford to produce rubber tires for the Ford autos. John Burroughs, a famous writer and naturalist, completed the group of campers. They called themselves the Four Vagabonds.

Each year, the group piled into cars and took a trip into the woods and mountains. The men were outdoors, but they were far from uncomfortable. Each had an army tent about 10 feet (3 m) by 10 feet (3 m). The campers brought a 20 (6 m) by 20-foot (6 m) dining tent. In this, they set up a collapsible circular table, 9 feet (2.7 m) across. They had a large supply of food and five helpers to set up the tents and prepare and serve the food. Edison even set up electric lights so he could read at night.

As these outings of industrial giants became known, reporters began to tag along. They wrote about the famous Vagabonds. The men had wood-chopping contests, rifle-shooting contests, and other races. They held discussions around the fire about politics, economics, and other subjects.

The Four Vagabonds' last trip was in 1924.

The two had known each other for some time. In fact, Ford had once been employed in one of Edison's companies. Ford and Edison got together with Harvey Firestone, a tire maker, and John Burroughs, a poet and author. The men called themselves the "Four Vagabonds" because they took a camping trip together every year.

During the 1920s, Edison became convinced that he could find a plant that would produce rubber. World War I had shown the need for American independence from foreign sources of rubber. Edison wanted to help in that effort. At the time, the sap from rubber trees was used to create rubber. The trees were mainly grown on large farms in South America or parts of Africa. Harvey Firestone had pioneered the use of rubber from these trees.

Working Hard

Even at age 70, Edison worked hard: "I'm still working eighteen hours a day on the average and sleeping four or five."[4]

Edison wanted to find a plant alternative that could be grown right in the United States. With his usual thoroughness, he began to experiment with different plants to see if their sap could be used for producing rubber. Even during his vacations with the Vagabonds, he tested different plants for their rubber properties. He eventually tested at least 13,000 different plant species. He finally narrowed his choice to a variety of goldenrod. Research and work on growing rubber from these plants continued for years, even after Edison had died. The rubber experiment finally ended when World War II (1939–1945) began. The U.S. government decided to pursue chemically created, rather than naturally grown, rubber.

Edison received many honors for his work, including the Albert Medal of the British Society of Arts in 1892, the John Fritz Medal of the American Engineering Societies (1908), entry into the Hall of Fame for Great Americans (1908), initiation into the National Academy of Sciences (1927), and the Congressional Gold Medal (1928) for his contributions to society. Ford held the "Light's Golden Jubilee" in 1929 for the fiftieth anniversary of Edison's electric light bulb. *Life* magazine named Edison Man of the Millennium in 1997.

On October 18, 1931, Thomas Edison died. The U.S. president at the time, Herbert Hoover, made a request of Americans. He asked them to turn off the lights in their homes for a short period. This act was a symbol of how much electric lights and electricity had become a part of American life, even then, barely 50 years after they had been introduced.

At the time of his death, Edison had earned more than 1,000 patents. He was the only person to ever earn at least one patent every year for 65 years, starting in 1869 and running until 1933, two years after his death.

Thomas Edison received many honors in his lifetime and beyond.

Henry Ford (left) and Thomas Edison

LIGHTING THE WAY
TO THE FUTURE

Thomas Edison is not the only important American inventor who ever lived. In fact, during Edison's lifetime alone—and certainly before and after—many people made inventions that contributed a great deal to progress. James Watt perfected the steam engine. Robert Fulton extended the idea of the steam engine to power ships. George Stephenson created a practical railroad. Samuel Morse invented the telegraph. Cyrus McCormick's crop reaper completely changed farming practices. Charles Goodyear figured out how to make the production of rubber practical. The Wright brothers flew the first heavier-than-air craft.

Most Difficult Invention

When asked which invention was his most difficult, Edison said it was "the incandescent light—that was the hardest and most important."[1]

In each case, however, these inventors concentrated mainly on one idea or area. One reason the number of Edison's inventions is so amazing is because his areas of interest ranged far and wide. The number of patents issued to him—1,093 to be exact—is more than that held by any other single inventor in U.S. history. It is difficult to exaggerate the influence his work with electricity alone has had:

> Edison threw open the door through which not only he but a host of scientists and inventors rushed to make discovery after discovery. ... Edison's vision of a universe run by

electricity has been fulfilled. Blackouts, when they occur, bring life almost to a standstill. It is possible to [imagine] a world without automobiles, airplanes, and natural gas, but to revert to an age without electricity would cripple civilization.[2]

In the 1920s, Henry Ford honored Edison. He believed Edison and his inventions formed the basis for modern business and industry, if not for the entire American society. He thought Edison had made the economic and working lives of workers, and society in general, much better. Ford noted that electricity had become the

Other Inventions

The electric pen: This instrument looked like a pen, but instead of ink, it held a needle. An electric motor drove the needle up and down like a sewing machine. As the pen moved, it made tiny holes in a stencil that was later mounted on a printing press. The press squeezed ink through the holes, recreating the person's handwriting. After a brief life, the pen was overtaken by more efficient copying methods, including the typewriter. In the 1890s, the electric pen became briefly popular again as the first electric tattoo needle.

The typewriter: Edison found perfecting the typewriter difficult. The most difficult part was keeping the letters in alignment. He worked on it with his usual focus until he was satisfied with its performance. The typewriter was found in nearly every office until recently, when computers became common.

The stock ticker: The stock ticker was invented around 1867 and used by Gold and Stock Telegraph Company. When more than one ticker was on a telegraph line, though, some of the printers could not keep up. Edison's improvements included a way to automatically reset the tickers if they fell behind. He created a keyboard for transmitting the messages. He also altered the machine so it used less battery power.

foundation for industry. He credited
Edison with making the entire
industrial system in the U.S.
possible. As he said,

> *Electricity as a servant of electrical utility*
> *began with Edison. No one has as yet*
> *been able to comprehend how far–*
> *reaching this use of electricity really is,*
> *for it goes through every phase of our*
> *lives.* [3]

Ford believed Edison's contributions
to electrical generation and
distribution could not be overstated.

Movies

In 1910, Edison described the future educational use of movies. He might have been thinking of his own school days far in the past: "Information conveyed [through movies] would be retained in memory, where days and weeks of dry reading would fail of accomplishment."[4]

Until useful electric lights were created, people could
work only during the day. With electricity, people could
work all night if they wished. Working longer could
allow people to earn more money, which they could
spend. This helped boost the economy. Before
electricity, industries depended mainly on water power
to run their tools. Factories were limited as to where
they could be set up because they had to be near a water
source. With electricity, factories could be built
anywhere—even far away from any source of water
power.

Along with expanding industry and making businesses more productive, electricity has had other effects on individuals and society. It has made life safer. For example, electric refrigerators preserve food longer, decreasing the number of food-related illnesses and food-poisoning cases. Electricity has made life easier. For example, household appliances like vacuum cleaners and clothes washers have cut down the time needed to do housework. They have allowed more people to have more free time to spend their extra money.

"I do not regard myself as a pure scientist, as so many persons have insisted that I am. I do not search for the laws of nature, and have made no great discoveries of such laws. … I am only a professional inventor."[5]

— *Thomas Edison*

Along with Edison's inventions, his creation of the invention factory has had far-reaching consequences. Modern research methods have been built on the basic idea Edison used, which is to conduct as many experiments as possible. Even if most of the ideas are dead ends, they at least let the inventor know what does not work. Edison tackled large problems by breaking them into smaller parts and assigning research teams to focus only on a specific piece of a problem. Earlier inventors, such as

Edison's life and work are on display at museums across the country.

Benjamin Franklin, invented things almost as a hobby. Edison proved that being an inventor could be a serious occupation. He showed it was possible not simply to earn a living by inventing but even to become wealthy.

In 1928, Edison was awarded the Congressional Gold Medal. Secretary of State Andrew Mellon said of Edison at the ceremony,

"I'll never give up because I may have a streak of luck before I die"[7]

— *Thomas Edison*

Edison is set apart as one of the few men who have changed the current of modern life and set it flowing in new channels. They belong to no nation, for their fame, no less than their achievements, [goes beyond] national boundaries.[6]

How could one man see things in such unique ways and simply create idea after idea? It may never be understood, but it can certainly be marveled at and enjoyed.

Thomas Edison's work with electricity has been far-reaching.

TIMELINE

1847	1859	1862
Edison is born in Milan, Ohio, February 11.	Begins work as a newspaper seller on the Grand Trunk Railroad.	Publishes the *Weekly Herald,* the first newspaper printed on a moving train.

1869	1871	1871
Forms an engineering firm in October with James Ashley and Frank Pope.	Edison's mother dies April 9.	Marries Mary Stilwell December 25.

1868

1868

1869

Moves to Boston in
March to take a job
with Western Union.

Applies for his
first patent, for the
electric vote counter,
October 13.

His first patent
is granted June 1.

1874

1876

1877

Installs quadruplex
telegraph in October
on Western Union
lines.

Starts a laboratory
in Menlo Park,
New Jersey, in March.

Begins using carbon-
rubber disks in
telephone transmitters
in October.

TIMELINE

1877	1879	1884
Demonstrates the phonograph for the first time December 1–6.	Demonstrates the first practical incandescent light bulb on December 31.	Mary, Edison's first wife, dies on August 9.

1894	1909	1915
The Sneeze becomes the first motion picture to receive copyright.	Begins manufacturing a nickel-iron storage battery.	Appointed to lead the Naval Consulting Board.

1886

Marries Mina Miller
February 24.

1886

Moves to Glenmont,
in West Orange,
New Jersey.

1887

Organizes the Edison
Phonograph Company
October 10.

1916

Takes first
camping trip with
Four Vagabonds.

1927

Organizes a
corporation to
research local
rubber sources.

1929

Honored by Henry
Ford for "Light's
Golden Jubilee"
October 21.

1931

Dies at Glenmont,
West Orange,
New Jersey,
October 18.

ESSENTIAL FACTS

Date of Birth
February 11, 1847

Place of Birth
Milan, Ohio

Date of Death
October 18, 1931

Place of Death
West Orange, New Jersey

Parents
Samuel Edison Jr., Nancy Elliot

Education
No formal education.

Marriage
Mary Stilwell, December 25, 1871
Mina Miller, February 24, 1886

Children
Marion Estelle, born 1873
Thomas Alva Jr., born 1876
William Leslie, born 1878
Madeleine, born 1888
Charles, born 1890
Theodore, born 1898

Career Highlights
Invented the phonograph and demonstrated it December 1–6, 1877. Manufactured a practical incandescent light bulb and publicly demonstrated it December 31, 1879.

Societal Contribution
Created a practical light bulb and the electricity generation and distribution system to bring electricity into many homes. Improved many electric devices, including the telephone and telegraph lines, which aided in communication. Invented the phonograph and kinetoscope, which made sound and video recordings possible.

Residences
Milan, Ohio; Port Huron, Michigan; Boston, Massachusetts; New York, New York; Newark, New Jersey; Menlo Park, New Jersey; West Orange, New Jersey.

Conflicts
Edison's work with electricity used direct current (DC), which he favored over alternating current (AC). Edison made efforts to show the public that AC was more dangerous than DC, and fought his associates, George Westinghouse and Nikola Tesla, on the matter. In the end, AC became the standard for distributing electricity.

Quote
"My philosophy of life is work, bringing out the secrets of nature, and applying them for the happiness of man. I know of no better service to render during the short time we are in this world."—*Thomas Alva Edison*

ADDITIONAL RESOURCES

SELECT BIBLIOGRAPHY

Baldwin, Neil. *Edison: Inventing the Century*. New York: Hyperion, 1995.

Cramer, Carol, ed. *Thomas Edison. People Who Made History* series. San Diego: Greenhaven, 2001.

Dyer, Frank Lewis, and Thomas Commerford Martin. *Edison: His Life and Inventions*. New York: Barnes and Noble Books, 2005.

Israel, Paul. *Edison: A Life of Invention*. New York: Wiley, 1998.

FURTHER READING

Anderson, Kelly C. *The Importance of Thomas Edison*. San Diego: Lucent, 1994.

Burgan, Michael. *Thomas Alva Edison: Great Inventor*. Minneapolis: Compass Point Books, 2006.

Delano, Marfe Fergus. *Inventing the Future: A Photobiography of Thomas Alva Edison*. Washington, D.C.: National Geographic Society, 2002.

Dolan, Ellen M. *Thomas Alva Edison: Inventor*. Springfield, NJ: Enslow, 1998.

Tagliaferro, Linda. *Thomas Edison: Inventor of the Age of Electricity*. Minneapolis: Lerner, 2003.

Web Links

To learn more about Thomas Edison, visit ABDO Publishing Company on the World Wide Web at **www.abdopublishing.com**. Web sites about Thomas Edison are featured on our Book Links page. These links are routinely monitored and updated to provide the most current information available.

Places to Visit

Edison Birthplace Museum
9 Edison Drive, Milan, OH 44846
419-499-2135
www.tomedison.org
Visit Edison's home in Milan, Ohio. Edison's great-great-great-grandnieces serve as tour guides to the historic site. Visitors can also see the Milan Canal.

Edison and Ford Winter Estates
2350 McGregor Boulevard, Fort Myers, FL 33901
239-334-7419
www.efwefla.org/home.asp
Visitors to the estates can see Edison's and Ford's vacation homes in Florida. Tours of their homes, gardens, and Edison's laboratory are available. Edison's inventions are on display.

Edison National Historic Site
Main Street and Lakeside Avenues, West Orange, NJ 07052
973-324-9973
www.nps.gov/edis/contacts.htm
Edison's Glenmont Estate houses his 29-room home, laboratory, greenhouse, and gardens. Visitors can see this historic site. A calander marks special events, tours, exhibits, and programs.

GLOSSARY

arc light
An electric lamp that creates bright light when a spark jumps a gap between two wires.

civil war
A war within a country between two groups that want power.

dynamo
A type of generator that converts mechanical power into electricity.

electric current
The movement of electricity through a wire.

electromagnet
A magnet formed when electricity flows through a coil of wire.

filament
A very fine wire or thread; in a light bulb, the filament glows and produces light.

generator
A machine that produces electricity by turning a magnet inside a coil of wire.

golden jubilee
The fiftieth anniversary of an event.

incandescent
Glowing with intense light and heat.

Industrial Revolution
A period of rapid industrial growth; in the United States, the Industrial Revolution began in the early 1800s.

low-grade iron ore
Rock that contains a small percentage of iron.

Morse code
> A pattern of dots and dashes that represent letters used in telegraphy.

patent
> A legal document giving an inventor sole rights to manufacture or sell his or her invention.

quadruplex telegraph
> A telegraph that can send up to four messages at the same time on one wire.

resistance
> The amount of opposition a substance gives to the passage of an electric current.

scarlet fever
> A highly contagious disease that occurs mostly in children; it causes a bright red rash, a sore throat, and high fever.

stock ticker
> A telegraph that transmits stock prices to stock brokers and bankers.

tasimeter
> A device used to measure very minor heat changes.

vacuum
> A sealed space from which all air or gas has been emptied.

Source Notes

Chapter 1. An "Enlightened" Inventor

1. "Edison's Electric Light." *The New York Times*. 21 Oct. 1879. On This Day. 2006. The New York Times Company. 7 Nov. 2006 <http://www.nytimes.com/learning.general/onthisday/big/1021.html>.

2. Ibid.

3. Thomas A. Edison. Letter to Dill Hays. 15 July 1930. The Edison Papers. Rutgers University, Piscataway. 10 Nov. 2006 <http://edison.rutgers.edu/images/xx/xx0055.jpg>.

4. Thomas A. Edison. Letter to Daniel H. Craig. 17 Dec. 1870. The Edison Papers. Rutgers University, Piscataway. 9 Nov. 2006 <http://edison.rutgers.edu/images/al/al0106.jpg>.

Chapter 2. Early Life

1. Thomas A. Edison. "Edison On the Labor Question." *Scientific American*. 5 Nov. 1887: 289.

2. Frank Lewis Dyer and Thomas Commerford Martin. *Edison: His Life and Inventions*. New York: Barnes and Noble Books, 2005. 20–21.

3. Neil Baldwin. *Edison: Inventing the Century*. New York: Hyperion, 1995. 20.

4. Ibid. 27.

5. Charles D. Lanier. "Two Giants of the Electric Age: I. Thomas A. Edison, Greatest of Inventors" *Review of Reviews*. Vol. VIII. July 1893. 44. The Edison Papers. Rutgers University, Piscataway. 18 Dec. 2006 <http://edison.rutgers.edu/imags/fp/fp0862.jpg>.

Chapter 3. Teenage Telegrapher

1. Neil Baldwin. *Edison: Inventing the Century*. New York: Hyperion, 1995. 32.

2. "New Aspects of the Art of Music." *Edison Diamond Points*. May 1917. 12. 1999. Library of Congress. 8 Nov. 2006 <http://memory.loc.gov/ammem/edhtml/MAY171.jpg>.

3. "Edison Views the World at Seventy." *Edison Diamond Points*. February 1917. 14. 1999. Library of Congress. 8 Nov. 2006 <http://memory.loc.gov/ammem/edhtml/feb1714.html>.

4. Thomas A. Edison. "Thomas A. Edison: Philosopher—The Great Inventor's Thoughts on Work, Women, Art, Life and the Hereafter." *The Golden Book Magazine*. 13 (1931): 78.

Chapter 4. Becoming a Full-time Inventor

1. Edison notebook entry. 31 Aug. 1871. The Edison Papers. Rutgers University, Piscataway. 8 Nov. 2006 <http://edison.rutgers.edu/search.htm>.

2. Neil Baldwin. *Edison: Inventing the Century.* New York: Hyperion, 1995. 35.

3. Frank Hanaford. Letter to Thomas Edison, 26 June 1871. The Edison Papers. Rutgers University, Piscataway. 10 Nov. 2006 http://edison.rutgers.edu/images/al/al0199.jpg>.

4. Neil Baldwin. *Edison: Inventing the Century.* New York: Hyperion, 1995, 50.

5. Ibid. 51.

6. Ibid. 56.

7. Thomas A. Edison. Letter to Charles Buell, 1 Dec. 1873. The Edison Papers. Rutgers University, Piscataway. 11 Nov. 2006 <http://edison.rutgers.edu/images/al/al0921.jpg>.

8. Matthew Josephson. *Edison.* New York: McGraw-Hill, 1992.

9. Thomas A. Edison. Letter to Daniel H. Craig, 7 Dec. 1870. The Edison Papers. Rutgers University, Piscataway. 9 Nov. 2006 <http://edison.rutgers.edu/images/al/al0105.jpg>.

Chapter 5. The Invention Factory at Menlo Park

1. Neil Baldwin. *Edison: Inventing the Century.* New York: Hyperion, 1995. 89.

2. Ibid. 88.

3. Thomas A. Edison. "Thomas A. Edison: Philosopher—The Great Inventor's Thoughts on Work, Women, Art, Life and the Hereafter." *The Golden Book Magazine.* 13. 9 Apr. 1931. 78.

4. Neil Baldwin. *Edison: Inventing the Century.* New York: Hyperion, 1995. 101.

5. Thomas A. Edison. "Mr. Edison's Views of Life and Work." *Review of Reviews.* 85. January 1932. 31.

Chapter 6. A Light Turns On

1. Letter to Theodore Puskas, October 5, 1875, quoted in Paul Israel, *Edison: A Life of Invention.* New York: Wiley, 1998. 173.

2. Charles D. Lanier. "Two Giants of the Electric Age: 1. Thomas A. Edison, Greatest of Inventors," *Review of Reviews.* Vol. VIII. July 1893, 44. The Edison Papers. Rutgers University, Piscataway. 18 Dec. 2006 <http://edison.rutgers.edu/images/fp/fp0862.jpg>.

SOURCE NOTES CONTINUED

3. "Edison's Electric Light." *The New York Times.* 21 Oct. 1879. On This Day. 2006. The New York Times Company. 7 Nov. 2006 <http://nytimes.com/learning/general/onthisday/big/1021.html>.

Chapter 7. Family Man

1. Neil Baldwin. *Edison: Inventing the Century.* New York: Hyperion, 1995. 255.

2. "Edison Views the World at Seventy." *Edison Diamond Points.* February 1917. 14. 1999. Library of Congress. 8 Nov. 2006 <http://memory.loc.gov/ammem/edhtml/feb1714.html>.

3. Kathleen McAuliffe. "The Undiscovered World of Thomas Edison," *Atlantic Monthly,* Dec. 1995.

4. Thomas A. Edison. Notebooks. 15 Jul. 1885. The Edison Papers. Rutgers University, Piscataway. 8 Nov. 2006 <http://edison.rutgers.edu/images/dl/dl0018.jpg>.

5. "Edison Family Album," *Edison National Historic Site.* 2006. National Park Service. 18 Dec. 2006 <www.nps.gov/archive/edis/home_family/fam_album.htm>.

6. Neil Baldwin. *Edison: Inventing the Century.* New York: Hyperion, 1995. 414.

7. Ibid. 261

8. Neil Baldwin. *Edison: Inventing the Century.* New York: Hyperion, 1995. 349.

9. Madeleine Edison. Notebooks. The Edison Papers. Rutgers University, Piscataway. 10 Nov. 2006 <http://edison.rutgers.edu/images/xx/xx0591.jpg>.

10. "Charles Edison." *Dictionary of American Biography, Supplement 8: 1966–1970.* American Council of Learned Societies, 1988. Reproduced in Biography Resource Center. Farmington Hills, MI: Thomson Gale. 2006. 8 Nov. 2006 <http://galenet.galegroup.com/servlet/BioRC>.

11. Charles Edison. Letter to Thomas Edison. 16 Oct. 1930, The Edison Papers. Rutgers University, Piscataway. 8 Nov. 2006 <http://edison.rutgers.edu/images/xx/xx0548.jpg>.

Chapter 8. The West Orange Years

1. Thomas A. Edison. Letter to James Hood Wright, August 1887. The Edison Papers. Rutgers University, Piscataway. 8 Nov. 2006 <http://edison.rutgers.edu/images/dt/dt0639.jpg>.

2. Neil Baldwin. *Edison: Inventing the Century.* New York: Hyperion, 1995. 193.

3. Ibid.

4. Charles D. Lanier. "Two Giants of the Electric Age: I. Thomas A. Edison, Greatest of Inventors" *Review of Reviews*. Vol. VIII. July 1893. 42. The Edison Papers. Rutgers University, Piscataway. 18 Dec. 2006 <http://edison.rutgers.edu/images/fp/fp0861.jpg>.

5. Neil Baldwin. *Edison: Inventing the Century*. New York: Hyperion, 1995. 85

6. "Who's Who in the Film Game," *The Nickelodeon*, 1910: 63. 1999. Library of Congress. 8 Nov. 2006 <http://memory.loc.gov.ammem/edhtml/nick1.jpg>.

7. Thomas A. Edison. "Why Do So Many Men Never Amount to Anything?" *The American Magazine*. 91. January 1921. 89.

Chapter 9. Later Life

1. Paul Israel. *Edison: A Life of Invention*. New York: Wiley, 1998. 415.

2. Matthew Josephson. *Edison*. New York: McGraw-Hill, 1992.

3. "Thomas Edison's Vision." Naval Research Laboratory. 11 Nov. 2006 <http://nrl.navy.mil/content.php?P=HISTVISION>.

4. "Edison Views the World at Seventy." *Edison Diamond Points*. February 1917. 14. 1999. Library of Congress. 8 Nov. 2006 http://memory.loc.gov.ammem/edhtml/feb1714.html>.

5. Ray Robinson, ed., *Famous Last Words: Fond Farewells, Deathbed Diatribes, and Exclamations upon Expiration*. New York: Workman Publishing, 2003. 3.

Chapter 10. Lighting the Way to the Future

1. "Edison Views the World at Seventy." *Edison Diamond Points*. February 1917. 15. 1999. Library of Congress. 8 Nov. 2006 <http://memory.loc.gov.ammem/edhtml/feb1714.html>.

2. Robert Conot. *A Streak of Luck,* New York: DaCapo Press, 1986.

3. Henry Ford and Samuel Crowther, *Edison As I Know Him*. New York: Cosmopolitan Book Corporation, 1930.

4. "Who's Who in the Film Game," *The Nickelodeon*, 1910: 63. 1999. Library of Congress. 8 Nov. 2006 <http://memory.loc.gov.ammem/edhtml/nick1.jpg>.

5. Thomas Edison. "Unsolved Problems that Edison is Studying." *Scientific American*. 8 Jul. 1893. 25.

6. Neil Baldwin. *Edison: Inventing the Century*. New York: Hyperion, 1995. 388.

7. Thomas Edison. Letter to Frank Hanaford, 26 Jul. 1869. The Edison Papers. Rutgers University, Piscataway. 8 Nov. 2006 <http://edison.rutgers.edu/images/al/al0014.jpg>.

INDEX

ABOUT THE AUTHOR

Charles Pederson is a consulting editor, writer, and translator. He has written or contributed to many publications for both children and adults. A graduate in linguistics, international relations, and German, he has traveled widely, bringing to his work an appreciation of different peoples and cultures. He lives near Minneapolis, Minnesota, with his wife, children, dog, cat, and frog.

PHOTO CREDITS

J. Walter Thomas/AP Photo, Cover, 3, 95; AP Photo, 6, 8-9, 11, 39, 51, 71, 80, 83, 87, 88, 97, 98 (top), 99; North Wind Photo Archives, 15, 34, 52, 61, 72, 96 (bottom), 98 (bottom); J.D. Pooley/AP Photo, 16, 96 (top); U.S. Department of the Interior, National Parks Service, Edison National Historical Site, 19, 34, 25, 26, 43, 44, 49, 62, 67, 79; Times Herald, Tony Pitts/AP Photo, 93